STORYSELLING

THE ART AND SCIENCE OF CREATING AND TELLING A STORY THAT GRABS ATTENTION AND GETS THE RESULTS YOU WANT.

First published in the UK in 2016

Copyright © 2016 John Rees

ISBN: 978-1-326-77158-4

All Rights Reserved. No part of this work may be reproduced without the permission of the copyright owner.

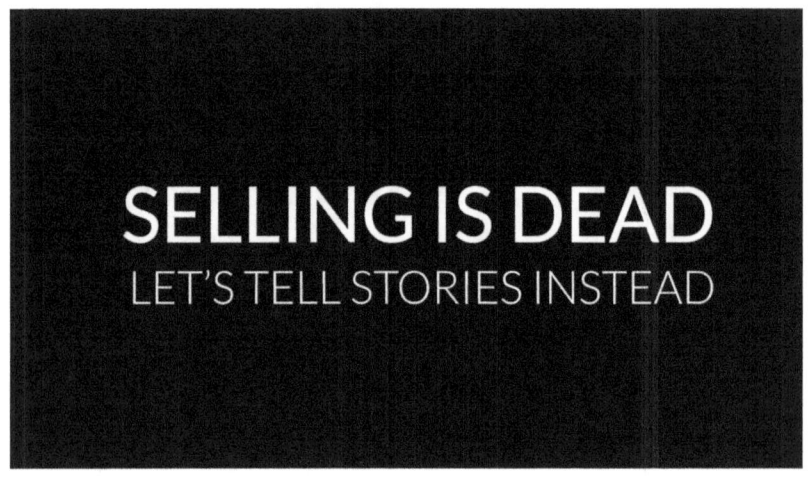

SELLING IS DEAD
LET'S TELL STORIES INSTEAD

We all know how hard it is to succeed in business today. There's so much competition for attention.

The way some people respond is to just sell harder.

But that's not going to work because the conventional approach to selling is broken. It doesn't work because buyers are far more informed than ever before.

That's why you must be smarter to prosper.

You need a new approach that places your audience right at the centre of everything.

You can't just push your product at people and hope they buy. must win them over by telling a story that'll grab their attention and motivate them to do business with you.

You need a new approach.

Welcome to StorySelling!

This is a softer, more intelligent approach to selling.

You frame your story in a way that makes sense to your audience. You think about their interests and then relate your story to that.

This is a fundamentally different to conventional selling that often relies on brute force and ignorance. Pitching a product and then using pressure to close a sale may have worked in the last century, but not today.

WHO IS THIS BOOK FOR?

Anyone who has a story to tell can use StorySelling to achieve results.

You could be in sales, marketing, customer service or any other role where you share information and want to influence someone's thinking.

You may want to close a sale or develop a partnership. And the best way to do that is through a story.

I will teach you the four most important things you need to now to master StorySelling.

WHY STORIES ARE IMPORTANT

Stories have been around a very long time. Throughout history, knowledge has passed from one generation to the next through stories.

Often these were embellished for dramatic effect and that's what made them so captivating.

They told of great deeds, of heroes defeating enemies. They became the stuff of legend.

They also created movements, formed religions and built great empires.

Stories are really powerful things.

And that's why there's such an interest in storytelling in business.

There's a massive (and growing) body of work on the neuroscience behind why stories are so compelling. But I'm not going into any of that, because frankly it's beyond doubt.

Stories just work because we love them. Think back to your childhood.

I bet you can still remember some of the stories your parents told you, or you learned at school. Stories stay with you. That's their power.

And that's why they're so important in developing business relationships.

In business, stories come in different forms.

You write a story such as a white paper, a sales proposal or an email.

You share your ideas in a discussion, lecture, speech or presentation. And if it's good it'll grab attention.

People buy you and your story first. Then they buy what you're selling.

That's because we all generally make a decision to buy based on how we 'feel' about something or someone.

This is the emotion.

Then we look for reasons to justify that decision.

This is the logic.

The emotion is created by the story and the way you tell it. It builds a picture in the audience's mind, that will motivate them to take some action.

So you must inspire and motivate your audience. You must tell them why they should care about what you're selling.

You must describe your unique difference.

And you do that with a story that's authentic, clear, concise and compelling.

APPLE LED THE WAY

Apple is a business that has always done this very well. When the late Steve Jobs introduced the latest 'i' device he didn't go into much technical detail.

He told us a story about why we needed the new thing he was selling.

He described what was wrong with the current way of listening to music on the go, making a phone call or using a computer.

He even poked fun at the companies who tried to sell us this (as he saw it) sub-standard stuff.

He built a very clear picture of what was needed to create a better future. Then he showed us how Apple had created that better future.

With a showman's flourish he unveiled the solution to the problem.

He described how wonderful our life would be now that we had this amazing thing at our disposal.

And the price? He always told us how much it would cost and when we could buy it. But by the time he'd finished his story, the price was irrelevant. We didn't really care how much it cost, because we just had to have it! People queued for days at Apple stores around the world to get their hands on the latest device.

That's the real power of inspirational stories that create overwhelming desire.

Some say that Steve was an amazing salesperson. And he was because he did the basic things very well.

Being a great salesperson isn't about applying pressure and using tricks to close a sale. It's far more subtle than that. It's about understanding motivation. Building a sense of anticipation, building desire and satisfying it.

Of course Steve didn't succeed all the time. In fact, he had a number of high profile failures. But his successes massively outweighed them. And he left a legacy that many would envy.

APPLE REINVENTS THE PHONE

iPhone. Iconic, desirable and hugely successful.

If you'd looked at mobile phones in the early 2000's you would have said the market was saturated. It was dominated by Nokia. The world didn't need another mobile phone.

Then in January 2007, Steve Jobs walked on to a stage and pulled an iPhone out of his pocket, and changed the world forever.

Apple reinvented the phone. And they succeeded because most mobile handsets were not great to use.

They had their own software and user interface. Moving from a Motorola to a Nokia for example, wasn't easy. You had to effectively learn how to use the new device from scratch.

Apple redesigned the hardware and user interface. They made it easy to use. And this helped them to dominate the smartphone sector they'd created.

The phone was transformed from a device to make calls and send texts to being the centre of our digital lives.

It became the standard way we consume information, stay in touch with friends, share news, photographs and videos, listen to music and work.

If you'd asked consumers what they wanted, the iPhone would probably have never been invented. That's because the real genius of organisations like Apple is to open our eyes (and wallets) to new possibilities.

They created the desire and motivation to buy.

They did this again with the iPad and continued to innovate.

It's only in recent years that the pace of innovation has slowed. Many think this was inevitable when Steve died.

Apple changed our relationship with technology because they focussed on what it meant to our life, rather than how it worked.

They don't sell features like FaceTime by describing how it works. They tell us how it keeps us in touch with our family and friends anywhere at any time. And very few of the people who use FaceTime know or even care how it works.

They just use it. And it just works.

I now want to give you another example of the power of a story.

This is an advert that's been hailed as one of the greatest ever made. It was daring, different, expensive and a massive gamble. It was also only ever shown once on national TV. It is the famous Apple 1984 ad.

NINETEEN EIGHTY FOUR (1984)

It's a date that conjures up powerful and evocative images in your mind.

Many of us instantly think of the George Orwell book that told the story of a dystopian future.

1984 is about mind control through propaganda. Big Brother is the figurehead leader who controls everything. Individualism is prohibited and independent thinking is regarded as 'thoughtcrime'.

The Thought Police uncover and punish thoughtcrime. They use surveillance and psychological monitoring to find and eliminate members of society who challenge the party's authority and ideology.

Many of Orwell's ideas have become reality or entered everyday language. "Thought Police" is widely used to refer to political and ideological correctness.

So this is the backdrop to the brilliant Apple Ad.

The 60 second commercial was shown only once on national TV in America. That was on January 22, 1984, during a break in the third quarter of American Football's Super Bowl Championship game.

That ad single handedly changed how the Super Bowl would be used as an advertising platform in future. It also cost around $800,00 which was seen as a huge gamble at the time.

When it was shown to the Apple board before being aired, they hated it. But Jobs won out and the ad was shown. The impact was significant.

The tagline was "Why 1984 Won't Be Like 1984"

It told the story of a future where Big Brother (IBM) controlled the way we think, act and use information.

With Big Brother, we all live in a world with no choice and total thought control. There is no flair, creativity or individuality. With Big Brother, nothing changes, ever.

If we 'Think differently' with Apple, we get freedom and individuality. We also unleash creativity and take human development to the next level.

In one 60 second vignette, it positioned Apple as creative, different and human, while re-positioning its competition as dull and controlling.

Now millions use iPhones, iPads and Macs. So some believe that Apple has become Big Brother.

But they will argue that at least you can now think for yourself. You can use thousands of apps to do wonderful things, unleash your creativity and express your individuality.

So I've described why stories are so powerful. And we've looked at how a master story teller such as Steve Jobs can effect massive change.

Let's now move on to talk about a structure you can use to create your own story.

STORY STRUCTURE

So we know that stories are very powerful. But how do you create a story that works?

Like many business owners, you may not know where to start. That's why you need a simple guide. And that's what I'm going to share with you in this section.

If you just start writing it's easy to ramble and get lost. It's like starting out on a car journey without planning your route.

You'd quickly get lost.

Having a simple structure makes the whole process easier and much more efficient.

When you write your story, you want it to be authentic, clear, concise and compelling.

Aim to get it on one page, which means no more than 500 words. You can always expand parts of it out later.

This will make it stand out and get noticed, which is exactly what you want.

So these are the four headings you will use;

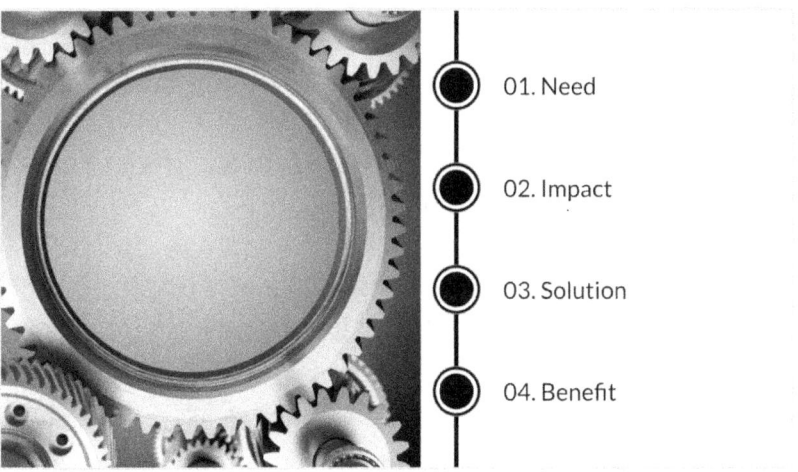

1. NEED

The starting point of your story is to describe the problem you solve or the opportunity you enable.

This is where you grab your audience's attention.

You're not trying to ram your product down their throat. You're addressing something that they care about.

Needs can be business and personal.

Typical business Needs include cutting costs, improving efficiency, managing risk, driving innovation, making more money, ensuring survival and complying with legislation.

Personal Needs include things like career advancement, personal wealth, health and well being, ego and personal gratification.

2. IMPACT

When you've defined the Need, describe what effect it has.

What happens if the Need isn't satisfied and what's the benefit of taking action? Or the bad thing that will happen of you don't.

The more profound the impact, the higher the motivation to act.

This is important because a Need that's not a priority isn't going to result in action. It's like one of those nagging things you know you should do. But because nothing bad will happen if you don't, it just drags on. You push it to the back of the queue. And eventually you forget about it.

If a problem could cause something bad to happen that threatens someone's career or the survival of their business, they will be motivated to act.

But what do you do if you address a Need your audience doesn't really know or care about?

Then you must create the Need.

This is what Apple did when it introduced the first generation iPod in 2001.

Portable CD players weren't great, I know because I owned several of them. They were cumbersome and you had to carry so many discs around. But they worked.

PEOPLE OFTEN DON'T KNOW WHAT THEY REALLY WANT, NEED OR DESIRE...

UNTIL YOU SHOW THEM

There were also some MP3 players around but they were difficult to use and upload music to.

So there was an opportunity to create a better way to listen to music on the move. And that's the gap that Apple exploited.

When Henry Ford introduced the first model T car in 1908, he wasn't responding to demand. He showed people how his new auto-mobile was better than the horse drawn carriage.

3. SOLUTION

When you've established the Need and Impact you can now position how you uniquely address it.

You must help the buyer understand what makes your Solution different to and better than the alternatives. This doesn't necessarily mean directly knocking the competition.

It means positioning your Solution in a way that shows why you are different to everyone else.

You can do this by saying something like;

> "Current Solutions have been around for many years. And because they are all based on the same model they all have the same shortcomings. We took a fresh look and decided that a different approach was needed. And that's why we developed our Solution in this way."

I'm sure you get the idea. You're not knocking any one competitor, but you are positioning yourself as being different.

And unless you do that, the buyer just regards you as another 'me too' idea. You become a commodity with no distinguishing features. And that makes it difficult to stand out.

4. BENEFIT

Being different is important, but only when it has a benefit attached. It's easy to create a benefit statement if you use the F.A.B. formula. This stands for Feature-Advantage-Benefit and it's a great way to identify the 'real' benefits.

Feature is the way something works.

Advantage is what it does better than the alternatives.

Benefit is the value it delivers.

For example;

Our new car has a hybrid engine (Feature)

This makes it 45% more fuel efficient than other cars (Advantage)

Which means that you save more than £1,500 a year on fuel costs (Benefit)

You may also want to add proof to support your claims. Customer testimonials have been used for centuries. That's because they work well. It's not that people think you're lying. It's just that you have a biased view.

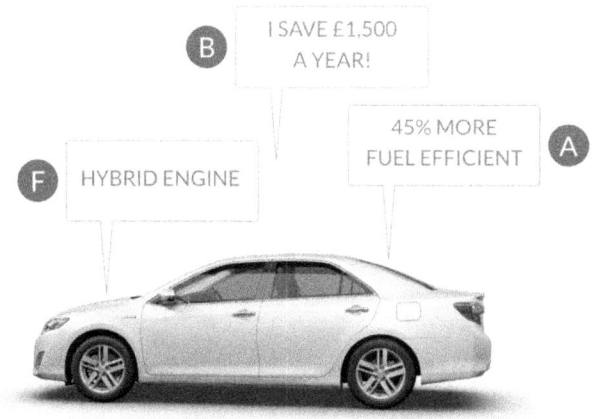

So when others endorse your claims, it's seen as an extra level of confirmation. And because humans are herding animals we often feel comfortable following the majority.

When you've created your story, you can use it in many different ways.

You can create a short version which we call a Power Summary. This is something you can use when someone asks you what you do.

Aim to keep this to no more than 50 words and ideally less. This is because you want it to be brief and memorable.

Rather than just explaining your role you describe the benefit of what you do. For example;

> *"I help small business solve the problem of poor cash flow. Late payment is a big concern and my unique service ensures you get paid on time every time."*

This Power Summary is 29 words long, but it plants a few ideas.

Cash Flow is a problem for most small businesses. And late payment is usually the cause. So this will be a Need that resonates with many business owners.

If I say I have a unique service that solves the problem, there's a fair chance they will at least want to know more. They will probably want to know what my service is and why it's unique.

So this should get the conversation started, which is exactly what you want. To get to 50 words or less isn't easy though. It takes work to edit and condense your story to the absolute core.

Many studies have shown that brevity is important. It's also common sense. If you bombard someone with too much information they start to glaze over. They have difficulty processing what you're saying and that's when they lose interest.

Being concise is hard to start with, but once you get into the habit of cutting the padding, you'll be surprised at what you can say in a few words.

IN SUMMARY

Describe the Need rather than talking about your Solution first.

Talk about the impact the Need has. If this is low or non-existent there will be little motivation to act.

For established Needs it's relatively easy.

In other cases you have to create awareness of the Need and then build the demand for it. This is typical where new Solutions are developed.

Then describe how you uniquely address the Need. Compare and contrast other approaches but don't directly knock the competition.

Lastly, talk about the benefits of your unique Solution. And remember to frame these in a way that makes sense to the audience.

Now you should understand how to create a story and condense it into a Power Summary.

IMPROVE HOW YOU WRITE

The best stories work because they motivate people to take action. And they do that because they have 3 simple features.

Clear means your story is easy to understand;

Concise means it's as short and detailed as it needs to be;

Compelling means it grabs attention and is irresistible;

The easier you make it for people to understand and be enthusiastic about your idea, the more successful you'll be. This is blindingly obvious but many people overcomplicate things.

Simplicity really is the essence of effective communication. This means cutting the padding and focussing on the core.

This has been acknowledged by some great thinkers and artists like Da Vinci who knew the value of simplicity and as he said "simplicity is the ultimate sophistication".

Chinese philosopher Confucius said "Life is simple but we insist on making out complicated". This isn't a literal translation, but it's close enough.

> Simple can be harder than complex: you have to work hard to get your thinking clean to make it simple. But once you get there you can move mountains.

And Apple is a company that prides itself on the elegance and simplicity of its solutions.

It take things out of their products to make them easy to use. Other companies add features because they think this provides a better experience, but it doesn't. It just makes it more difficult to understand.

The way to achieve simplicity in a story is to edit it ruthlessly. You must get to the absolute core by using as few words as possible.

Start by eliminating those 'filler' words that don't actually mean anything. They just bloat your story and make it more long-winded and confusing than it needs to be.

As well as padding, there's also jargon, buzzwords or slang. These are in common use today but they just complicate messages and confuse people.

Avoid cliche's, jargon and management speak such as "Blue sky thinking .. Touching base ... Leading edge ... Reaching out to you and Paradigm shift".

These are so over used, tired, outdated and they have little, if any impact other than to irritate people.

Don't use complex words just to sound smart, because this often has the opposite effect; it can make you sound pretentious, which turns people off very quickly.

Minimise the use of superlatives and don't make outrageous or unbelievable claims you can't substantiate.

Be economical with the words you use. Instead of writing 'At this present moment in time' just say 'now'. Instead of 'A large number of' use 'many'.

'A joint collaboration' becomes either 'joint or collaboration' because a collaboration is a joint initiative.

That's why it's useful to check the literal and actual meaning of words and any that can, must go!

There's real beauty and elegance in a story that's crisp and minimal but still conveys the exact meaning you intend.

Here's another example;

> "I am seeking to find a new career at this current moment in time"

This is 14 words long and it can easily be cut to 5.

> "I want a new career"

You see, this has nine fewer words and it's a far crisper and more direct phrase.

Your aim is to create the strongest mental picture possible through your words. Edit ruthlessly to eliminate any words that do not add value and clarity.

Also avoid repetition because this adds padding you don't need.

For example;

> 'The latest poll showed that 33% or 1 in 3 voters said they would vote for the Conservatives at the next election.'

Why do you need 33% and 1/3?

They are the same thing said differently. This is unnecessary repetition. Use one or the other but not both at the same time.

When you do these things, your story will become clear and concise.

It becomes compelling when you describe the unique benefits you deliver. I talked about this earlier so revisit it if you need a reminder.

Developing a clear, concise and compelling story does take time and patience. You may have to break habits you've formed over the years.

But stick with it, because the effort will pay off. You will see things differently and become a far more compelling and successful story teller.

TELLING YOUR STORY

The first part of this book concentrated on how you develop your story. This section will look at how you communicate it.

If you want to succeed in business you must be able to present your story to an audience.

You can tell your story in many different ways, through different channels. The most common way is to give a presentation. This could be face to face with a small or large audience. It could also be via an online meeting or even a pre-recorded event.

However you do it though, the principles are the same.

But many people have a real problem with this. They avoid it or get someone else to do it. That's because they either get nervous, or they don't think they are a 'natural communicator'.

Both of these are excuses.

The reason you may get nervous is usually because you are not prepared. You are scared of saying the wrong thing or making a fool of yourself.

This is very common and it's easy to fix and I'll show you how in the rest of this book.

Presentations are everywhere but too many of them are still bad. There are many reasons for this but the biggest problem is lack of creativity and an ability to think visually.

It's just easier for some people to crack out slides filled with text, than it is to think of visual metaphors to really make a point.

They don't think about telling a story, they just think about pitching their product or service AT the audience.

This is despite the fact that we all know that we retain information far more effectively when we see a memorable image.

The two areas that cause problems are story design and delivery.

Bad design means that your story doesn't flow well.

Your slides probably don't look very good. They are crammed with text. Images are poor quality and very much an afterthought.

Maybe you're also trying to get too many points across on each slide.

Overall it's confusing, dull and boring. It's just doesn't come across in a very clear concise or compelling way.

No wonder you're nervous! I would be too because this isn't a great starting point.

But things can get a lot worse. Because if the design is bad, what happens next could spell disaster. That's because poor delivery compounds the problem.

I remember many events, but one has always stuck in my mind. I won't mention names, but it was a classic example of what happens when things go wrong.

It took place in a room with about 30 people. The presenter wasn't really prepared. He thought he'd just play it by ear and hope for the best.

He started badly and it went downhill from there.

Because he had literally thrown a slide set together, there were no images. It was slide after slide of bullet points. He sensed the audience losing interest, so he tried speaking faster.

He started looking more frequently at the slides, and less at the audience. Then the kiss of death. The thing every presenter and audience member truly dreads. He started reading every bullet point on every slide. His tone became flat and monotonous.

The audience murmured and then he faced the slides and ignored them for the rest of the presentation. When it was over he turned and smiled weakly and then left.

I was in the audience, and I can tell you it was very uncomfortable for him and embarrassing for us.

We all wanted it to end, but being British I guess we thought we should see it through.

This is unfortunately a true story. I've seen other mediocre and poor presentations, but it doesn't have to be like this.

There is no real excuse, it's just laziness.

Anyone can be a good story teller if you put in the effort. So just bear that person in mind, and commit to improving what you do. Follow my advice and I guarantee that you will improve the way you present your ideas.

WRITING THE PRESENTATION

Your story is the starting point of any presentation.

Forget the slides and the way they look for now. Get the story straight first and the rest will follow.

The first thing to do is to be clear about what your 'Big Idea' is. This is the key topic you'll talk about. It's the one thing you want the audience to remember.

- What is it that you want to share that you think will make the audience sit up and take notice?

- How will it truly 'rock their world'?

- What will they remember when it's finished?

Your goal is to describe this in less than 50 words. If you can't, it's either too complicated or you don't understand it.

Here are some examples to illustrate the point;

> "How to increase sales revenue by 45% in 12 months using social media to drive targeted marketing campaigns."

> "The principles of quantum physics explained in 2 minutes - No Phd required!"

> "The psychology of the laws of attraction and how you can harness them to enhance your credibility, build your appeal and advance your career."

I'm sure you get the idea. And when you've nailed this, you will create a headline that summarises it perfectly. This will be the title of your presentation, and to attract attention it must be clear, concise and compelling.

Unfortunately, too many people give this little thought so they produce stuff like;

> "Presentation to …Discussion on …Overview for …"

These are deadly boring, uninspiring and hardly likely to get the heart pumping. They don't actually say anything. They are not headlines, they are placeholders.

An overview is meaningless because it has no context or impact. It's dull, non-challenging and generic. It doesn't tell me why I should care!

Dump the boring titles, make sure the headline grabs attention and you have an excellent starting point.

Here are a few examples of headlines that would work well;

- 6 guaranteed ways to increase sales by 45% in a year.

- 3 proven ways to attract high value clients.

- The 4 laws of attraction and a new you.

- How to create messages that never fail.

- Learn quantum physics in 10 minutes.

I know we live in a politically correct time but don't be afraid to take a few risks. So be bold, be different, offer a fresh perspective and you will attract attention.

PRESENTATION STRUCTURE

There are 3 parts - introduction, key topics and the close.

Introduction

Introduce yourself and tell them what you're going to talk about. Run through your agenda and give them a high level summary of each section. Also tell them how long it's going to take.

Key Topics

This is your chance to demonstrate your expertise by showing you understand the issues they are or should be concerned with. Then you can describe how you uniquely provide a solution.

The Close

This is where you bring everything together and seek their commitment.

When you've done this, you can now break the story into slide-sized chunks. Group it into logical segments, which will typically be topic areas.

Also make sure you limit the number of ideas you share on each slide.

I wouldn't be too worried about the number of slides. I'd be more worried about putting too much information on a single slide.

More on that later.

I'm not suggesting you learn your presentation parrot fashion, but the very act of writing and splitting it in this way will load it into your memory.

If you're creating a presentation to record and place online the approach above works very well.

If you're presenting to a live audience there are two other things to think about.

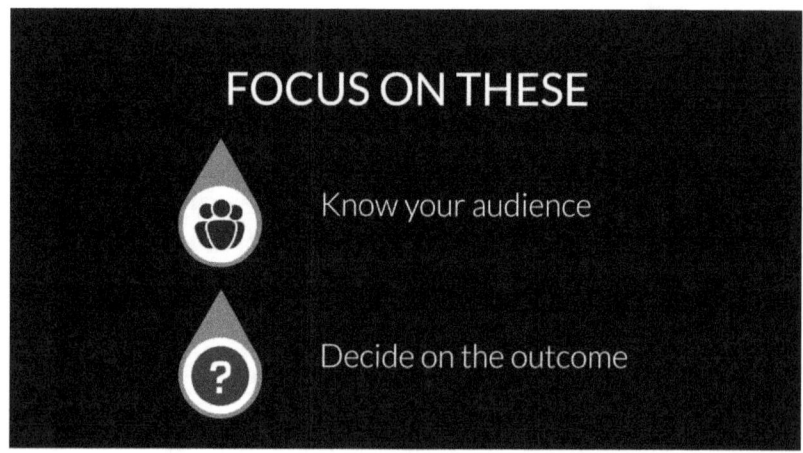

1. Know your audience

This is crucial because by understanding their interests, you can personalise your story to grab their attention and keep it.

The best way is to always put your audience first. That doesn't mean you don't promote your solution. It's just that you present it in a way that satisfies the audience's needs first.

The key things to think about are;

- Who is your audience?
- What do they care about?
- What's their level of understanding?
- What will grab their attention?
- What's their expectation?

If you are presenting to a small group, build a profile of each person. What does it tell you about them and their interests? How can you use this information in your story to make it more interesting for them?

2. Decide on the outcome

This simply means being clear about what should happen after the presentation has finished. So you start designing it with the end in mind.

If it's an introduction to your company, they will want to learn about what you do and how you can help them.

You will want to show that you understand their needs, and have the expertise to provide an excellent solution.

If it's a final session, they will want to know why they should select you. And you will want to give them compelling reasons to do business with you.

When your desired outcome aligns with the audience's, your chances of success are dramatically improved.

So you've crafted your story. You're happy it hits all the key points. You know what you want to achieve.

Now you're ready to pull it all together and design excellent attention grabbing content.

DESIGNING THE CONTENT

Designing a presentation is more than just choosing a template, colour scheme or font.

It's not just about style. It's about providing a better user experience which makes it easier for the audience to understand your story and get excited about it.

If you've ever suffered from Death by Powerpoint, you'll know that it's not much fun.

You sit there, bored out of your mind as the clock seems to drag by. You're thinking about anything other than what's being said. You zone out and start doodling or checking Facebook or email. In fact, you're probably doing anything except listening to the presenter drone on and on and on. You just want it to end.

So the last thing you want to become is a Death by Powerpoint presenter. And if you follow my advice, I promise that will never happen. Of course I can't absolutely guarantee that you'll become a 'rock star' presenter overnight. But I can guarantee that if you follow these simple rules, you'll take major steps in that direction.

This advice is based on my own personal experience of giving hundreds of presentations over many years. So I'm helping you to avoid some of the harsh learning experiences I've had!

There are many books written about how to design and deliver great presentations. They go into a lot of depth.

They discuss colour theory, cognitive psychology and other areas that explain how we respond to messages.

I'm not going into any of that. I'm going to keep it as simple as I can. In fact, I'm going to focus on 6 pillars that I know will make an instant improvement in the way you design a presentation.

1. Simplicity

2. Clutter

3. Words

4. Images

5. Composition

6. Effects

For the best results you must lock all six in place because they compliment each other. If you only do a few you will get sub standard results.

1. Simplicity

This is the essence of clear communication because the simpler something is, the easier it is to understand.

But simplicity doesn't mean 'dumbing down' and losing valuable content just to be brief.

As I said earlier, it means distilling your story to the absolute core, and removing anything that doesn't help understanding.

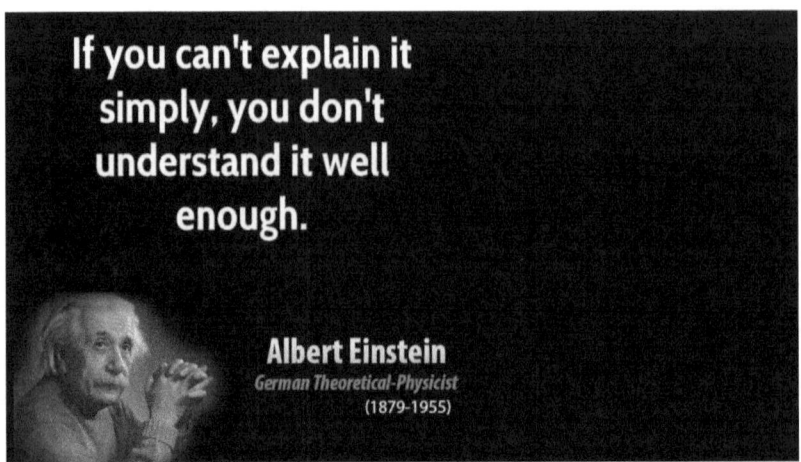

The ability to say more with less is a skill you must develop. And the more you understand your subject, the better you'll be able to do this.

Look at each slide in your presentation and ask yourself 4 questions;

    1. What's the purpose of this slide?

    2. What message or idea do I want to get across?

    3. How can I make the point with fewer or even no words!

    4. Is there a stunning image that can get my idea across?

Be careful not to overdo it though, because you must find the right balance. And this depends on your story, the audience and the purpose of the presentation. A complex technical subject will obviously require some detail, but avoid padding because this leads to information overload even for the brightest people!

I often get asked 'How many ideas should I put on a slide?' And the answer is simple. It's one.

This is backed by cognitive research, which proves that when you give someone information in easily digestible chunks, their retention and recall is vastly improved.

Keep it relevant and simple and you have the first pillar in place.

2. Clutter

This is the enemy of simplicity. It's anything that doesn't add value to the message, or make it clear and easy to understand. The biggest culprits are things like company logos, slogans and copyright notices.

These are annoying, and they cut down on the available space you can use for the really interesting stuff. Unfortunately this is common practice, but why do you need your company name and logo on every slide?

What does this actually add? And how does it help the audience get excited about your message?

Most people put it on as a matter of habit but it's rarely necessary. If your story is in the public domain it's not confidential is it?

If you are sharing confidential information that's not in the public domain, it's a good idea to have the audience sign a non-disclosure agreement. But keep the slides free for the really important things you want the audience to remember. And only show your company name and logo on the first and last slide.

Cut the clutter and the second pillar is in place.

3. Words

A presentation should be mainly visual. Think about it as a film documentary. It's a story that you tell with images to keep the audience interested.

If it's crammed with words, it's a report, so you should hand it over to the audience to read!

The most common way people use text is with the dreaded bullet point. You see them everywhere, because people fire up their presentation software and just enter text. This is their idea of developing a presentation and it's sloppy, unprofessional, lazy and the major cause of 'Death by Powerpoint.'

Of course you do need some words, but keep them to a minimum. Also make sure that you use words that have real impact. Cut 'filler' words and jargon.

Commit to using words sparingly and creatively and your third pillar is locked in.

4. Images

A powerful image can make a far bigger, and more lasting impact than words alone. And the more relevant and concrete the image is, the more powerful the effect.

That's why an image should not just be decorative. It should say something. It should be a visual metaphor for the idea you want to get across.

And this is where you have to be creative.

You must decide what you want the image to represent. An easy way is to think of a keyword and search online. You'll get millions of suggestions. But be careful because some images have become visual jargon. After all, how many lightbulbs have you seen on a slide?

These are the easy choices to make, but if everyone else has them no-one will remember you.

So you need to think of something different.

If you want to talk about inspiration and you can't think of another metaphor other than a lightbulb, pick a different type of lightbulb. Or create one yourself.

Another approach is to take your keyword and put it though a thesaurus. I use this a lot and it gives you much more scope to be inventive. You then have much more to chose from and a better chance of being different.

The golden rule here though is to always use high quality images. Cheap or free clip art images do not look good. They definitely scream 'amateur' so avoid them at all costs.

There are many great sources of reasonably priced stock images such as Alamy, Fotolia, iStockphoto and Shutterstock.

Make sure that your images are superb because this is the fourth pillar you must have in place.

5. Composition

This means placing your content on a slide in a way that makes sense to the audience.

A good way to do this is to think like a photographer, designer or artist. They use various techniques for framing their subjects to make them more interesting.

One such technique is called the Rule of Thirds.

The basic idea is to break a scene into a 3 x 3 block grid and then place the subject at key points of interest, rather than the default setting of dead centre.

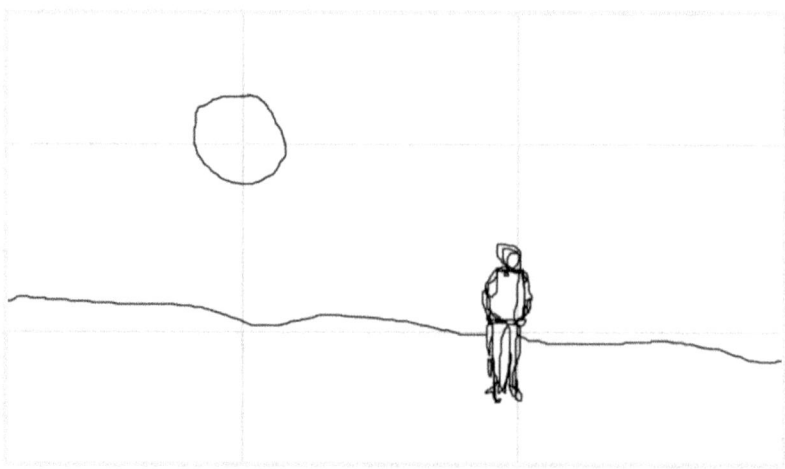

You could place the image top right, bottom left, filling a slide or even 'bleeding' over an edge. There's no right answer on composition, so experiment and see what looks best.

'White space' is another technique that works well.

This isolates and frames a word, phrase or image for maximum impact. It's great for focussing attention and it can also look elegant and sophisticated.

As well as using space to isolate and frame, you should also consider the space between related items. Make sure it's obvious which image and item of text go together, so they are viewed as a group rather than random elements on a slide.

There is no absolute right or wrong answer on composition, but some things definitely work better than others. This is where creativity comes in. So look at what others have produced and use these ideas as inspiration.

However, 'rules' exist to be broken, so have some fun and experiment to find what works best for you.

Composition is the fifth and critically important pillar because it's how your content is presented.

6. Effects

The sixth and final pillar gets many people excited. They just seem to get carried away with the special effects and sounds they can add with Powerpoint, Keynote and other presentation software.

But be very careful. Unless these are used wisely, you can end up with sensory overload as objects slide in on a comet flash and slides explode from one to the other.

I'm sure you've seen this many times, and the novelty wears off very quickly.

Simplicity dictates that you don't complicate things by adding distracting clutter. And special effects can be a major cause of clutter.

Before you go live with any special effects, ask yourself how they make it easier for the audience to understand your story. And how do they help you put your message across in a better way.

I personally prefer simple fades between slides or subtle dissolves. This works well and it always gives a presentation a sophisticated and professional look.

SLIDE DESIGN

Here's how I'd handle this slide.

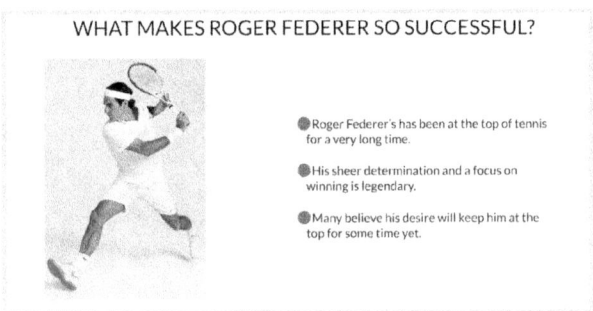

See the difference? Roger is one of the most famous people on the planet, so I wouldn't even add his name. I'd also ditch all the text other than the 3 words that tell the real story 'focussed on winning'

He is the story so I'd make the image full sized and by aligning a headline within his field of vision, you emphasise the 'focus' part of the message even more.

This is an idea for a slide layout for an entire presentation. The simple quote marks and line are the container for your content. This forces you to minimise words because too many will look really bad!

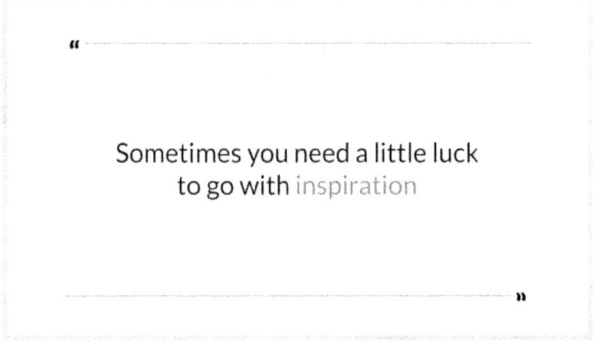

You can also think creatively and use a different colour to isolate a key word. This idea can also work well with a black background.

By thinking about the message and rephrasing the words, you get a slide people will remember and it gives you far more scope to expand on your idea. Instead of 2 lines of text you've created a memorable 'formula'.

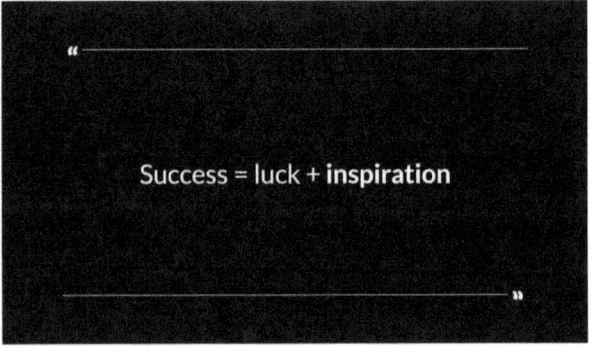

You can also use the theme to frame an image..

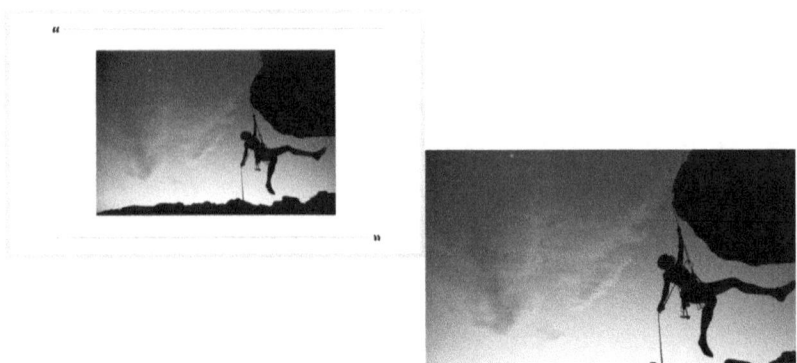

This slide talks about what drives innovation.

So rather than using a standard boring headline or plain text, you can play around with a few ideas to make even that appealing. The audience is far more likely to remember this than the lines of text and cramped image in the first slide.

StorySelling

Let's look at how you can eliminate bullet points
On this slide there's a lot to take in.

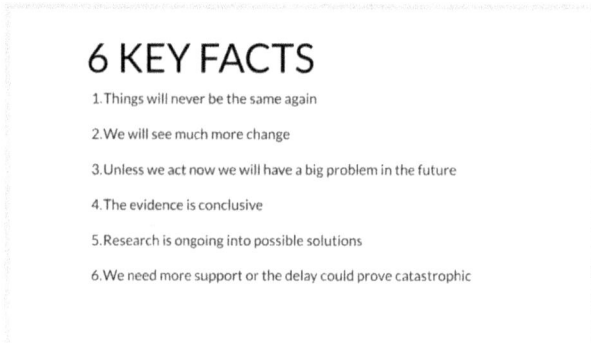

So let's split it across 6 slides, like this. The only thing that changes is the text in the speech bubble and a simple fade takes care of this.

This is a classic introduction slide that's boring because it lacks impact.

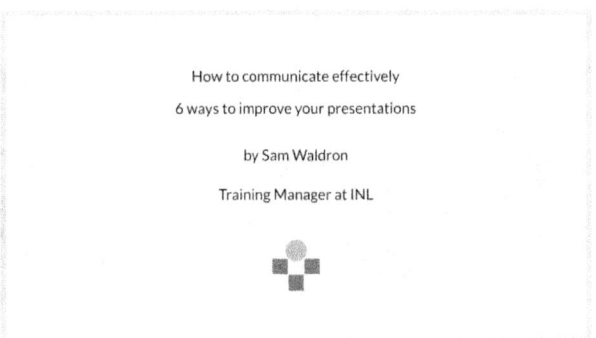

I've reworked it to make it more appealing and obvious what the presentation is about. I've used different sizes and colours in the font to add emphasis. This looks crisper, easier to read and far more professional.

Here we may be talking about attitude. The glass half-full / half-empty is a well know metaphor we easily relate to.

This shows how white space can work. By using a non-standard font you also create something more interesting and memorable.

This looks bad. The image is in a white box against a darker background. It looks small, isolated and out of place.

I've added emphasis by freeing the image from it's box and using it as a pointer to the message to create a more spacious, easily understandable and professional look.

Morbi non erat non ipsum pharetra tempus. Donec orci. Proin in ante. Pellentesque sit amet purus. Cras egestas diam sed ante. Etiam imperdiet urna sit amet risus.

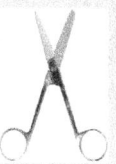

Morbi non erat non ipsum pharetra tempus. Donec orci. Proin in ante.

StorySelling

FONTS

Futura Medium
ABCDEFGHIJKLMNOPQRSTUVWXYZ
abcdefghijklmnopqrstuvwxyz
1234567890

Futura Medium Italic
ABCDEFGHIJKLMNOPQRSTUVWXYZ
abcdefghijklmnopqrstuvwxyz
1234567890

Futura Condensed Medium
ABCDEFGHIJKLMNOPQRSTUVWXYZ
abcdefghijklmnopqrstuvwxyz
1234567890

Futura Condensed ExtraBold
ABCDEFGHIJKLMNOPQRSTUVWXYZ
abcdefghijklmnopqrstuvwxyz
1234567890

WHY FONTS MATTER

The kind of font you use determines how your slide design looks. Obvious I know, but many people pay no attention to fonts at all. If you just use whatever is 'standard' in your presentation software, you are missing a big opportunity to be different.

To most people fonts are pretty insignificant. Yet to their devotees they are the most important feature of text. But fonts are not just for geeks.

Selecting a font determines the kind of message and image you want to convey. And today there are more than 200,000 different fonts to choose from!

The first thing to decide is do you go for a sans serif or a serif font?

The difference is that a serif font has stems or extensions to a letter as shown here. A sans-serif doesn't have any stems. So why does that matter?

Ultimately it's about readability and recognition. And as you'd expect, opinion is divided about what works best!

There are some things you shouldn't use - especially those 'fun' fonts such as Curlz MT - unless of course you specifically want to convey that kind of image. The IBM logo just wouldn't look the same would it? This is an extreme example, but I'm sure you get the point.

I'm not going into detail bout typography here because this is a specialist area. There are people who design fonts for a living and they pay incredible attention to even the tiniest detail.

What I will say is that you must pick fonts that look good and convey the right image. Then you want to use them consistently in all the content you publish. But don't get too hung up on this, otherwise you'll end up with "font paralysis" because there are just too many to choose from.

You can mix serif and sans-serif but restrict this to headlines and body text. This just looks cleaner and remember, the aim is to make it really easy for the audience to understand your message. Simplicity is what you are striving for and you must reflect this in your design and choice of fonts.

As you look at these font families, you'll also notice that they have different weights. Some have hairline, light, regular, medium, bold, extra bold, black, and italic options for all the above!

If you really like a font you can add variation to your work by using different weights, for example;

GILL SANS BOLD (14 point)
Gill Sans Regular (14 point)
Gill Sans Light (14 point)

There is no shortage of choice and new fonts are being released all the time.

I'm not trying to turn you into a professional typographer here, but you should pay attention to selecting fonts that work for you.

DELIVERING A PRESENTATION

So this is where it all comes together. This is where you deliver the story that will really captivate your audience and get the right results.

> Are you nervous?
>
> Do you have butterflies in your tummy?
>
> Are you thinking about what could go wrong?

If you are don't worry, it's normal. It's also a healthy sign because it shows that you care. The trick is to harness this energy and use it to help you perform well.

I'm going to give you some simple ideas and techniques that you can use to make sure you use your nervous energy to give a great performance every time.

We are often led to believe that great communicators are born.

Martin Luther King, Churchill, John F Kennedy and Steve Jobs are seen as natural performers who could easily captivate an audience.

It is a fact that some people have more innate and natural skill than others, but the truly inspired communicators have something else.

Superstars in any walk of life harness their talents through total conviction and self belief coupled with a dedication to being the best.

Churchill was widely regarded as a wonderfully natural orator who could speak without notes. He was highly intelligent, charismatic and undoubtedly had great genes. He was born into the British aristocracy and politics was in his blood. His speeches were said to come straight from the heart. Whilst he was a gifted orator, he nevertheless wrote his key speeches and practiced in front of a mirror until he was word perfect. This meant that he was able to make his delivery appear very natural.

Apple CEO and founder, the late Steve Jobs, was truly obsessive and his legendary drive for delivering the perfect pitch drove his people crazy.

He fussed over the most minute detail. He would always work himself and others very hard to make sure that everything was just right.

Lights would be positioned and sequenced to shine at just the right angle, at the right time, to show just how gorgeous a product looked.

Music was specifically selected to create the right atmosphere. And the story was planned with military precision to flow perfectly.

When showtime arrived, Steve was all California cool, relaxed and talking to the audience as though they were having a chat over coffee.

There are also many great examples of his presentations online and it's worth taking the time to see him at work.

Although not everyone can join this band of iconic communicators, you can improve dramatically by following some basic steps.

The most important thing to remember about a presentation is this ...

It's a performance

Unfortunately many stories are the same. They are predictable, dull and boring.

It's your job to enthuse your audience and get them excited about your story. And the best way to do this is to make it engaging, entertaining and rewarding for them.

You can do this by injecting your own unique personality into this because the way you say something is as important as what you say.

That's why you must add **Sparkle** to your presentation. Unfortunately, you can't buy Sparkle in a packet. It's the combination of things you must do to bring your story alive.

Star quality

Pace

Attitude

Respect

Knowledge

Length

Engagement

STAR QUALITY

So you've designed a story that's capable of captivating your audience. But it's not a movie with a soundtrack. It doesn't stand on its own and tell the full story. It needs a narrator to bring it to life. And that's you!

You are the essential ingredient that makes the whole thing come alive. **You are the Star of the show!**

You are the centre of attention and the audience is keen to hear what you have to say.

Some people are obviously more extrovert than others, so they feel more comfortable being the centre of attention.

But being the star doesn't mean jumping around and showing off. It means being engaging and commanding attention in a way that your audience will respond to.

You must develop a presence and a style you feel comfortable with and then practice it until it becomes natural.

Here are a few of the things you can do to build some of that star quality;

1. Demeanour

The audience takes it cue from you, and this sets the mood.

If you are dour, very serious and grumpy looking, they will normally adopt a similar mood. And if they do, this gets the story off to the worst possible start.

By creating a friendly and personable environment, you can make an immediate connection with the audience.

When you smile and are pleasant, people will frequently mirror you. This puts them at ease and it also makes you feel less stressed and nervous.

And it's a fact that if they like you, they will be more inclined to give you a fair hearing.

But make sure this is genuine. Phoney smiles slip easily and if the audience think you are not being honest, you will lose the ability to influence them.

I'm not suggesting you grin like a Cheshire Cat throughout though. This will be irritating and people may think there's something wrong with you!

Get yourself into a positive frame of mind and genuinely look forward to it. Then start with a smile and an "I'm glad to be here" attitude and posture. This sets the right scene and you can build from there.

2. Movement

Being stuck behind a podium is my idea of hell. You are almost chained to this thing which becomes a crutch for you to lean on. A bigger problem is that it's a barrier between you and the audience.

That's why I'd advise against using a podium out of choice. It's far better to move around, because you can make more of a connection with the audience. Depending on the layout of the room, you can even walk amongst them.

When you move around you can also release some of the nervous energy that's coursing through your body. And that's an important factor in helping you to relax and perform well.

But beware of constant motion because you then become less of a focal point and more of a moving target! Also be careful about invading someone's space and getting too close. This can be distracting and make some people feel uncomfortable.

A good rule of thumb is to move and then stand still for a short while when you are speaking. Then move over to another area and do the same. By mixing it up in this way, you can easily connect with all sections of the audience.

3. Eye contact

When you smile and move, make sure you connect with the audience in a genuine way. Choose a few friendly faces and focus on them.

Try to identify groups in different parts of the audience as you move.

Look for faces on the left, the right, at the front, back and in the middle. When you do this, you connect widely, rather than talking to one part of the audience, or even worse, one person!

Obviously if you have a small group you have the opportunity to connect with everyone.

4. Mistakes

We all make them and when you do, try to minimise their impact. Don't over-react or tell lies.

In fact, you can make light of this, but don't get stressed because this only makes things worse.

If someone points out that you've made a mistake, don't get into an argument. You could stand your ground if you are absolutely certain of your facts, or you could say "I'm pretty certain of that, but I will check it later." Then you move on.

If you've hit a mental block, be honest. Owning up makes you more human. And if you've developed a great rapport with the audience, they will understand and forgive you.

By displaying honesty with an audience your credibility and trustworthiness will rise. They will then be even more open to your ideas.

5. Practice

This is the most important thing you can do because it has a massive impact on your confidence and competence.

You can practice anywhere at any time and here are some ideas you can use;

- Pitch your story to a group of colleagues or friends you trust to give honest feedback.

- Ask them to make notes and look for areas you can improve.

    - How well did you set the scene and open?

    - Did you establish a good rapport with them?

- Did they feel involved in the pitch, or was it just a monologue?
- How well did you cover the subject?
- How good were your slides?
- How well did you handle questions?
- Did you excite and inspire them?
- Did they believe you?
- How well did you close?

- Record your story and listen to it over and over.
- Visualise by closing your eyes and running through it in your head.
  - Notice how you open and establish rapport;
  - See yourself confidently covering each point;

- See heads nodding in agreement to the points you make;
- Listen to the applause when you finish and the words of thanks.

- Video yourself to see how you look and perform. Play it back and notice what you do well and what can be improved.
- Pay attention to the way you move, connect with the audience and deliver your message.
  - Look at your body language - what does it tell you?
  - Remember how you felt at each point and what you were thinking;
  - How did you look?
  - How did the audience respond?

Be critical but constructive. No-one is ever perfect so don't get hung up on small details that really don't matter.

The objective after all is to become the best communicator you can be. And minor flaws can be distinctive and endearing.

Don't eliminate what makes you unique.

Take a tip from professional entertainers who have honed their skills and leave the audience screaming for an encore. Now I'm not suggesting you do a song and dance act, but you should think about how you can make your story pitch truly memorable.

PACE

Your voice is your main asset so you must use it correctly.

However, if you have a heavy accent and you speak too fast, people will find it hard to follow what you are saying. And if they can't follow you, they will lose interest.

That's why you must set the right pace, tone and clarity with your voice.

Great communicators seem to be relaxed and comfortable. They act and speak in a measured and controlled way. They don't gabble or speak at a million miles an hour. You can understand every word they say and you follow the story easily.

Pace is versatile because you can use it in different ways. If you want to emphasise key points, you could speak more slowly and deliberately.

You could also increase the volume and repeat a phrase a few times. You could also lower your voice to a whisper and force the audience to listen harder. But whatever you do, always make sure you can be easily understood.

Practice will help you set the right pace, and that's why you should experiment if you are serious about improving your skills.

If you are nervous you can get yourself into the right frame of mind by doing something as simple as breathing.

Inhale deeply and exhale slowly.

Relax your body and run through the opening in your mind. Then when it's showtime you'll be ready to perform.

ATTITUDE

This is important because the way you approach an audience and project yourself determines your success.

If you have a positive and upbeat attitude you stand a great chance of carrying your audience with you.

When you inject your unique personality and combine it with real passion, genuine enthusiasm and expert knowledge, the results are consistently good.

Enthusiasm is infectious and the more positive you are about your subject, the better it comes across.

Positive words and confident body language will heavily influence an audience and get them on your side.

To keep them on your side, make sure your enthusiasm is proportionate and don't overdo it.

Remember, the aim is to present your ideas, not become a crazed evangelist who preaches at people.

I've seen so many people deliver 'standard' corporate overviews that they clearly don't believe in.

They just go through the motions and their ambivalence shines through. They are bored, they are boring and they get the results they deserve.

The key is to find the right motivation. When you are clear about why you are doing it, developing the right attitude becomes easier.

RESPECT

Respect is powerful because it means that people will open their minds as well as their ears and eyes.

They will listen deeply, because they regard you as someone with interesting (and possibly unique) ideas. They see you as an authority, a thought leader, who is worth listening to.

But you can never demand respect from people. You must win it through your personal and professional qualities.

And if people like you it's easier to win their respect. This means being open, approachable, fair and honest. It means having something different to say and injecting your own personality into it.

You can also win respect by giving it.

Listen to what people think and allow them to voice an opinion, even if it's at odds with your own.

Be courteous at all times and never try to score points by discrediting the other person's viewpoint.

If you do have a difference of opinion, state your case and try to win them over with the force of your argument and your personality. People will respect a robust debate and a strong defence of a viewpoint.

They will never respect a bully who shouts someone down and tries to prove them wrong.

KNOWLEDGE

Know your stuff. It's that simple!

If you want to be respected as an authority, never ever try to fool the audience. You will be found out and it'll be painful and embarrassing.

It's your responsibility to make sure you understand your topic and can talk around the story. During my career in the software industry, I remember many pitches given by salespeople who clearly didn't know what they were talking about.

When they were asked questions they deferred to a more informed colleague to give an answer. I've seen many highly paid '"parrots in suits" and it's not acceptable.

This still happens today, and that's why salespeople are often treated with contempt. They are regarded purely as the person who agrees the deal and closes the sale.

They are not seen as an authority, they are just the people who handle the paperwork.

- If you are a salesperson and you want to improve your effectiveness, educate yourself.

- If you run a sales organisation, you must invest in educating salespeople. The more they understand about what they are selling, the more effective they will be.

- If you are presenting an idea, make sure you know it inside out.

- If you are selling a concept, make sure you've thought it through so that you can talk with authority.

Confidence is a big factor to successfully tell a story and a key component of confidence is knowledge. Acquire it and prosper, or try to 'wing it' and you risk failure.

LENGTH

Attention spans are variable and some people just drift off after a few minutes, especially if you bore them.

Studies have shown that concentration levels really dip after 15-20 minutes and based on my experience, this is far shorter especially with senior people.

The more senior someone is, the less likely they are to just sit there and feign interest.

A few years ago I was advising a technology business. One of their goals was to expand into North America, and we had identified potential partners to do this with.

One organisation arrived with a team of 3 senior people. They were pitching their proposal and I had assembled a team of 6 from our side, including the CEO. He is a direct, no-nonsense type of person who hates wasting time.

Because I know him well, I briefed the potential partner on how they should approach this pitch. They partly listened but they decided to take a slightly different route. They thought they knew better. They didn't.

It lasted 7 minutes!

The CEO interrupted the person in full flow, stood up and said two words, then he walked out.

"Not Interested" was delivered with a finality that allowed no comeback.

They'd completely blown it by talking about their company, their experience and everything except my client and his needs.

If they'd got to the point faster we may have partnered with them. The moral of the story is this;

- Establish a connection immediately;
- Start with the audience's interests and not yours;

- Avoid padding and unnecessary small-talk;
- Get to the point and do it fast!
- Keep it brief;
- Be focussed and always try to finish early'
- Leave time for question.

ENGAGEMENT

Unless you are giving a formal speech, you must get your audience involved.

Always make a connection and establish rapport as fast as possible because this starts to build connections on a conversational and emotional level. Both of these are important because you want the audience to buy into your ideas and feel connected to them.

Steve Jobs did this amazingly well. You could hear the gasps and groans as he unveiled yet another new product or service that had the faithful in raptures.

You can engage your audience by moving around, smiling and making eye contact as we mentioned earlier. You can also do it by asking questions.

There is a time and a place for asking questions though. Some people like to do it at the end because they want to get through their story uninterrupted.

Others are more comfortable doing it at any time, because they have total confidence in their subject.

There is no right way and as ever, it depends on your judgement of the audience and what you feel most comfortable with.

ABOUT ME

I'm a business coach and mentor and for more than 30 years, I've worked around the world and generated hundreds of millions in sales. I've worked across industry sectors such as IT, consultancy, manufacturing, supply chain and sustainability.

This experience is built into my "Simple Success Strategies". These help ambitious businesses succeed by doing the right things.

You can see my ebooks, training courses, blogs and podcasts at www.reinventingthesale.com.

www.ingramcontent.com/pod-product-compliance
Lightning Source LLC
Chambersburg PA
CBHW072218170526
45158CB00002BA/645